The Lord Rules

P15

the Lord Rules-

Let's Serve Him!

Meditations on the Psalms

LESLIE F. BRANDT

Concordia Publishing House

St. Louis   London

Concordia Publishing House, St. Louis, Missouri
Concordia Publishing House Ltd., London, E.C. 1
Copyright © 1972 Concordia Publishing House
Library of Congress Catalog Card No. 72-80783
International Standard Book No. 0-570-03137-0

MANUFACTURED IN THE UNITED STATES OF AMERICA

Contents

Preface

This is the third volume of contemporary psalms that are based on or patterned after the psalms of the Old Testament. The first volume, *Good Lord, Where Are You?* portrays the insatiable hunger of the psalmist, or the 20th-century Christian, for God, and his perplexities and frustrations as he grapples for some sense of God's presence and power in this discordant world. The second volume, *God Is Here — Let's Celebrate!* places the major emphasis on the praise psalms — manifesting the confidence that "God is here" and is calling upon His children to celebrate this in word and deed. This third volume picks up all of the Old Testament psalms not included in the first two volumes and reinterprets them to portray what the feelings and attitudes of a 20th-century Christian may be in respect to his own worth, his nation and his world, and God's purposes for him in his day-by-day sojourn through this world.

Today's Christian, like the ancient psalmist, can honestly and openly express his doubts and perplexities to his loving God. At the same time he can lay claim to God's promises and demonstrate his faith in celebration of His presence in the world today. While his doubts resolve into joy and celebration, he acknowledges God's ownership and commission for his life and dedicates himself to service.

The Lord rules — let's serve Him!

LESLIE F. BRANDT

Psalm 15

Who is the one, O Lord, that remains a part
      of Your kingdom?
What are the prerequisites for membership
      in Your family?

It is that one who walks circumspectly —
    and in obedience to Your precepts and principles.
He must be open and honest before God and man.
He must speak and act in love toward his neighbor.
He cannot condone that which is evil
      and must not participate in that
      which promotes injustice.
He must listen to his brother's griefs
      and complaints.
He must seek to lighten his burden
      and to share in his sorrow and pain.
He must reach out to heal rather than to hurt,
    to be kind and gentle to all who cross his path.

Those who lovingly relate to God and fellowman
      will never be separated from the family of God.

Psalm 17

I cry to You out of desperation, my God.
Listen to me and judge me if I am in error.

I have honestly tried to do Your will,
    to promote Your causes, to speak Your Word.
I have avoided the pitfalls that have victimized
      so many about me.
I have acted in love rather than in anger.
I have never raised my hand in violence.
I have walked in the paths You have set before me.

And yet I am tripped up by despair.
There are great walls that I cannot break through,
    dead ends that lead nowhere,
     people to whom I cannot relate.
I reach out in concern and am rebuked with scorn.

I am weary, Lord, weary of well-doing.
I am tired of the reactions of those
      I seek to serve.
I seriously wonder if it is all worth it.

Grant me, O God, a measure of ecstasy.
Help me to feel good about myself
      and about my role in Your service.
Reveal Yourself in some special way this night
      that I may rest in joy and in peace.

Psalm 23

The Lord is my constant companion.
There is no need that He cannot fulfill.
Whether His course for me points to the
      mountaintops of glorious ecstasy
   or to the valleys of human suffering,
   He is by my side;
   He is ever present with me.
He is close beside me when I tread the
      dark streets of danger,
   and even when I flirt with death itself,
   He will not leave me.
When the pain is severe,
   He is near to comfort.
When the burden is heavy,
   He is there to lean upon.
When depression darkens my soul,
   He touches me with eternal joy.
When I feel empty and alone,
   He fills the aching vacuum with His power.
My security is in His promise to be near
     to me always,
   and in the knowledge that He will never
     let me go.

Psalm 26

I am about to make an important decision, Lord,
    and the day before me is charged
        with uncertainty.
Enable me to sense Your presence,
    to feel Your undergirding power,
    to be assured of Your guiding concern.

I have been Your son and servant for many years.
Even in my youth I claimed Your redeeming love
    and dedicated my life to Your purposes.
And from that time until now
    I have shunned the enticements of this world,
    the human ambitions that so teasingly beckon,
    to pursue Your objectives
        and carry out Your commands.

I have been faithful to the hour of worship
    and the time of prayer.
I have celebrated Your gifts of love
    and sung Your many praises.
My dearest friends are those who love
    and serve You.

And now, O Lord, I have come to a fork
    in the road.
I don't know which way to turn.
I commit this day into Your hands.
I pray that it may be lived by Your direction
    and in accord with Your will.

I raise my voice in thanksgiving, O God,
    for You have granted to me the assurance
        that You will guide my faltering steps.

Psalm 35

It is not easy, Lord, to follow after You.
While You take the hard road with joyous
      leaps and bounds,
  I stumble over every stone
    and slip into every rut.
You calmly weather each storm
     and walk fearlessly through the night.
I am buffeted by the winds,
    and I falter in the darkness.

And You always have answers, Lord,
  for those who confront You.
My tongue is thick and clumsy.
I cannot articulate what I feel
  or what they need to hear.
You have the wisdom and the power
     to meet the needs of men about You.
But I am foolish and ineffective,
  and my brothers turn away from me in disgust

I have really tried to relate to people about me,
  to reach out in love and concern.
I have shared their sorrows and their joys.
I have shelved my ambitions to respond to
    their needs.
But when I fail to produce what they want,
  or when I am limited by my humanity
    and incapacitated by my personal problen
  they will have nothing to do with me.
I feel as if I have been used only to be abused.
I am squeezed dry and then cast aside
    as if I were of no further value.

Yet I must continue to follow You, O Lord.
It is a hard path to walk,
  and I will falter at times.
I long intensely for an occasional oasis
  along this journey through wind and sand.
I need desperately Your touch of joy and enrichment
  as I labor amidst the blood and tears
  of this distorted world.
I am empty, Lord enable me
  to sense Your fullness
 and grant me the grace and the courage
  to be faithful as Your son and servant.

Psalm 45

My heart is full of joy today.
I reach almost frantically for the sounds
     that might express that joy,
   the words that would proclaim the exuberance
     that I feel at this moment.
I am heavy with praise,
   and I must express it lest I succumb to it.

You, my dear friend, were the channel of this joy.
You touched me with love and awakened
     my sleeping heart to the beauty
     and the fragrance of life about me.
God reached out through your devotion and concern
     to kindle anew a fire within me,
    or to fan the old embers into flames
     of light and passion.
You marched into my jungle of despair
     and made a path for me to walk in once more.
You sliced through my confusion
    and gave order and motivation
    to my purposeless gropings.

I am so very grateful — to God and to you.
I pray that God may use me,
   as He has so abundantly used you,
   to transmit joy to the joyless,
     despairing lives of His children
     who cross my path.
And I pray that God may bless you and keep you
     and use you forever.

Psalm 48

How great is my God!
He soars above our poor intellects like a
     snow-capped mountain over
     a sun-baked desert.
He scatters the profound theories of wise men
     like leaves pushed around by a winter wind.
He shatters the assembled might
     of world governments as an earthquake levels a city.
He reaches down in tenderness to earth's poor
     creatures and draws them to Himself.

Consider with me the greatness of my God.
Measure His judgments;
   embrace His eternal love.
Stand tall in your faith and courageous
     in your commitment,
   for He is truly a great God.

Psalm 51

O God, may the measure of Your eternal love
    be the measure of Your mercy.
And may the measure of Your mercy
    be sufficient to blot out my great sins
    and cancel out the guilt of my wrongdoing.

I have failed, O Lord, and my failures weigh
    heavily upon my heart.
I cannot share them all with my brother lest
    they weigh too heavily upon him
    and may even threaten my relationship with him.
But You know what they are, O God,
    and how far I have fallen short of Your
    standards and expectations.

I am only human, Lord.
It was not by my choice that I was propelled
    into this fractured world.
The weaknesses that plague me are not all
    of my doing,
    nor can I handle them by my strength alone.

I know that nothing can be hidden from You.
I can only acknowledge my indictment
    and accept Your loving forgiveness.
Purge me of my guilt, O Lord;
    heal the hurts of those
    who have been afflicted by my failures.

Revive my flagging spirit, O God.
Restore to me the joy and assurance of a right
    relationship with You.

Reinstate me in Your purposes, and help me to
avoid the snares and pitfalls along the way.

It is only then that my tongue will be set free
to sing Your praises
and my hands to perform the tasks You have
set before me.
It is only then that I can relate deeply
and meaningfully to my brother
and communicate to him the message
of reconciling love.

I bring You no oblation or sacrifice, my God,
only a foolish and self-centered heart.
I do come to You with a sincere desire to be
Your servant,
to walk in Your course for my life,
to receive Your love, and to channel such love
to my fellowmen about me.

I thank You, God, that this is acceptable to You
and that I will remain Your son forever.

Psalm 52

There are many clever people who apparently
      have no need for God.
With their keen wits and sharp tongues
      they seduce their fellowmen and use them
      to promote their own selfish ambitions.
They barge around in this world as if they owned it
      and have no consideration for those they
      hurt in the process.
They brashly step on one another in their avid
      pursuit of riches and power.
They scorn those they brush aside and destroy
      those who stand in their way.
They flaunt their achievements before men
      and brag about their self-sufficiency.
They demean those poor fools who support
      and applaud them in their ascent
      to their worldly thrones.

They will be toppled,
    these men and their thrones of clay.
From the dust they came;
    to the dust they shall return.
Their cleverness will dissolve into emptiness.
Their boasting will become like a hot wind.
Their achievements shall become as nothing,
    and they shall grovel before the victims
      of their atrocious acts.

This is not so with the child of God.
He may never know earthly success.
He may never be satiated with temporal riches.

But he is eternally secure in the love of His God.
Like a green tree that spreads its boughs
      to shield the weary traveler
    or holds out its fruit to the hungry stranger,
    he quietly and perpetually carries out God's
      purposes in a barren land.

Psalm 56

O God, I have tried incessantly to transmit
     Your love to people about me.
I shared my possessions; I gave of my time;
    I used Your gifts given to me to support,
      to help, and to bless others
      who were in need.

But I feel as if I had been used, O God.
People have wiped their feet on me.
They take what I offer and then go their way
     totally oblivious to my problems and pains.
They act as if I were in debt to them —
    as if it were my duty to share myself
     with them.

But even as I groan in complaint, O Lord,
    I know that this is Your course for me.
Even as they use You, so they will use me.
Truly, O God, I have nothing to lose,
    for it is in losing that I truly find that
     which is of everlasting value.

You are aware of my frustrations,
    my feelings of emptiness and loneliness.
You have promised to replenish my vessel,
    to make me a channel for Your eternal springs.
I am in debt, O Lord, to suffering humanity
    about me.
I must be emptied again and again —
    only to be filled
     from Your boundless resources

and then to pour out once more
Your blessings
upon those who need.

You have delivered me from the wasteland of need.
Therefore I dedicate myself anew to the task
of channeling Your gifts to the parched
lives of others.

Psalm 58

My heart grieves, O Lord, over the leaders
      of this world
      who play god with the lives of men.
With the clever twisting of half-truths
      they gather followers into their folds
      and manipulate them into carrying out
      their purposes.
They blind men to personal conscience and
      responsibility
      and enslave them to the wishes and
      ambitions of the state.

Then there are starry-eyed mystics who assume
      they are God's special gift to mankind
      and who,
    through devious tricks or inscrutable gifts,
    create their little cults of loyal disciples.

You shall have the last word, O God,
    and those who take Your place,
    or who stand in Your way as You seek
      to draw men to Yourself,
    will be subjected to Your judgments.

You are my God, almighty and eternal.
Forbid, O God, that I should ever turn from You
      to follow the false shepherds of this world.

Psalm 59

Deliver me, O God, from the enemies of my soul.
I am no longer afraid of men who stand in my way,
    even of those who obstruct Your purposes and who
        deceive their fellowmen with their arrogant
        and clever clichés.
They anger me, but they do not frighten me.
My pain and confusion come by way
        of my own weaknesses and faithlessness.

I strive for success and am fractured by failure.
I reach for ecstasy
        and am clobbered with depression.
I wait for guidance
        and Your heavens are gray with silence.
I ask for infilling
        and am confronted with emptiness.
I seek opportunities
        and run into stone walls.

I overcome these pernicious demons
        in the morning —
    only to face them again when day turns
        into night.
They refuse to die, these persistent devils.
They plague my days and haunt my nights
        and rob me of the peace and joy
        of God-motivated living.

And yet, O Lord, You have surrounded my life
        like a great fortress.
There is nothing that can touch me save
        by Your loving permission.

My faith will falter at times,
    but You will never fail me.
Teach me, O God, how
        to live by Your Word and promises,
    to sing Your praises,
    to carry on within Your purposes
        despite these taunting,
            tempting enemies of my soul.

Psalm 60

You made us, O God, a great nation.
The lands beyond our own tremble at our
      awesome might.
The rich wine of material wealth dulled our senses.
The tyranny of things obscured our vision.
We grew arrogant, self-satisfied,
    and were often insensitive to the needs
      of Your creatures beyond our borders.

We waved our swords menacingly at the potential
      enemies of our great country.
We established our outposts in the very heart
      of the enemies' camps.
We extended our powerful tentacles into other
      nations' undeveloped resources and
      drew their blood into our own.
And we did this in Your name, and we convinced
      ourselves that it was by Your will.
Now our defenses have been broken down, O Lord.
Our fortress has been breached.
We have given birth to offspring that threaten
      us from within.
Oppressed people within our boundaries are
      rising up to assert their identity.
Our disillusioned youth are rebelling against our
      hypocrisy and our insensitivity to human
      needs and rights.
Foreign philosophies are permeating our culture
      and our thinking.
Our self-centeredness has boomeranged
       and threatens to smother us in our own waste.

We are becoming paralyzed by fear and polarized
         by the extreme actions of radical
         and reactionary men.

Your Word is clear for those who would follow You,
    O God.
Your promises are assured for that nation that
    will worship You.
The enemies that threaten us and
    the problems that beset us
    can be absolved only in our returning to our God,
    and in allowing Him to guide us and through us
         to bless the world about us.
We seek Your help, O Lord, in restoring our great
         nation to those roots from which it came.

Psalm 68

We long for the day when God will take over
    our cities,
  when wickedness shall be suppressed
  and selfishness subdued,
  when people will begin to care for one another.

There will be clean air to breathe
    and pure water to drink.
There will be better schools for the young,
  hospitals for all who are ill,
  and jobs for those who seek them.
Everyone will feel needed and loved in such a city:
    the child, the laborer, the executive,
      the senior citizen.
There will be dignity and freedom and equal rights,
    whatever one's ethnic or economic backgrounds.
There will be homes to live in
    and parks to play in.
There will be libraries and theaters
    and halls of learning.
There will be a place for everyone to live and work
    and learn and rest and play.
And people will have time for one another.

O how we will praise God in such a city!
Our voices will join in a great chorus of celebration.
We will daily offer up thanksgiving to our God,
    who rules over our city.
And everyone will have time for one another.

But God does not rule over our cities.
Our streets are pregnant with crime.

The poor and the dispossessed are packed
        into ghettos.
Our schools are overcrowded and inadequate.
We choke on the air we breathe.
We stumble over our own litter and waste.
We neglect the old and ignore the young.
We rush pell-mell from pillar to post.
And no one cares for one another.

You seek, O God, to rule over our cities.
You have given us pure air and green hills
        and great forests and clean rivers.
You have showered upon us Your abundant gifts —
    all that we need to make our cities bright
        and beautiful.
And You have given to us Your love
    and the responsibility to care for one another.

This has been our great failing, O God:
    we have sucked to our individual bosoms
        the gifts of Your love,
    but we have never really learned how to
        care for one another.

You have rebuked us for our selfishness, O Lord.
We are smothering in the waste of our
        self-centered living.
Deliver us, O God,
    restore to us those cities in which You dwell,
    and teach us, our loving God,
    how to care for one another.

Psalm 78

It would be good for us to consider God's dealings
      with men and nations throughout history.
We ought to know these things;
    we have heard them again and again.
But we forget so quickly,
      and we fall so foolishly into the same pitfalls
        of infidelity and purposelessness.

God reached down and gathered a people for Himself.
He drew them into His fortress of love.
He revealed Himself to them
        through His commandments
        that taught them how to live together in peace.
He enabled them to sense His presence
        in miraculous ways.
He poured out upon them all that was needed
        to sustain them.
Even in the barren desert
    food was rained upon them from heaven
    and water burst forth out of the very rocks
      around them.
He sent them prophets to teach them
    and warriors to guide them
        through enemy country.
Like a shepherd who watches over his flock,
    our Lord watched over His children.

But like silly, confused sheep,
    the children of God went astray.
They became self-sufficient and wandered off
        to pursue their own selfish interests.

Many of them rebelled against their God.
And God, in His love, had to let them go because
they refused to accept His love
and to walk in His paths before them.

They became lost in the desert.
They suffered sorely for their sins.
They were hungry and thirsty and afraid.
Only then did they remember
the Creator of their youth
and the loving care of their heavenly Father
in those days when they walked in His paths.

Some of them turned back to God again.
They discovered once more their loving God,
a God willing to forgive them and accept them
and to gather them once more into His
fortress of love —
to care for them and watch over them like
a shepherd over his flock.

Like silly, selfish sheep,
we often wander off on our own,
imagining that we can find our own way
to joy and security.
We discover pain
and emptiness
and meaninglessness
outside the orbit of God.
We are out of joint,
and the deepest longings of our hearts
go unfulfilled.

I return, O God, to You and Your purposes
for my life.
I find You waiting for me,

ready to forgive my foolishness and my
rebelliousness
and eager to reinstate me in Your family
and reconcile me to Your will once more.

I thank You, O God,
for drawing me back to Your loving heart.

Psalm 79

Why is it, O Lord,
   that the ungodly appear to be so successful?
They have no use for the church.
They play fast and loose with the lives of others.
They live solely for themselves and have no
         concern for others except to use them to
         further their personal ambitions.
They not only obstruct Your purposes, God,
   they pollute Your world and taunt Your servants.

Why do You let them do it, O Lord?
Why don't You avenge Your enemies?
Why don't You show them through Your faithful
         servants that we are on the right course,
   that success comes to those who love
         and follow You?

Help me, O God, to love Your enemies even as You
         love them,
   to bear patiently and graciously their scorn
         and to serve You faithfully whatever
         the consequences.
Help me to measure my worth and success by
         Your standards
   and to rejoice in Your love and acceptance.

Psalm 83

I am so depressed tonight, O God.
I feel as if I am the sole target of an
    enemy barrage —
      that all the demons of hell are bent upon
      damning my soul for eternity.

I remember Your precious promises,
    but I do not witness their fulfillment.
I talk to people about Your love,
    and they drown my zeal with scorn.
I step forth to carry out Your will,
    but I feel no sense of accomplishment.
I mouth words, wave my arms,
    and beat the air with fruitless endeavor.
Then I fall like a wounded warrior,
    bone-weary, defeated, and lonely.
And I wonder if You are truly my God,
    and if I am really Your child.

Consume, O God, these demons that depress,
    these enemies that plague my soul.
May the whirlwind of Your Spirit
      sweep them out of my life forever.
May I awaken in the morning with a heart
      full of joy,
    and with the strength and the courage
      to walk straight and secure in the dangerous
      and difficult paths before me.

Psalm 87

This world is God's world.
And our great God loves the world that He made
　　and the beings that He created to dwell
　　　　upon it.

The black people, the brown people,
　　the yellow and the white,
　　those with slant eyes or straight noses,
　　the rich and the poor,
　　the lowly born and the nobility,
　　they are all God's people,
　　　　and His love embraces each and every
　　　　one of them.

Not all the creatures of this world
　　　　are citizens of the kingdom of God.
The people who shun His redeeming love
　　　　cannot inhabit the city of eternal light.
They become the children of darkness.
They shall wander forever through
　　　　the limitless spaces of nothingness
　　　　and emptiness.

The sons and daughters of God are those
　　　　who relate to their Father and Creator,
　　who walk in obedience to His will and His Word.
They shall dwell together in joy
　　and shall sing and dance in perpetual
　　　　celebration in that beautiful city beyond
　　　　the boundaries and borders of this
　　　　present world.

Psalm 89

I feel like singing this morning, O Lord.
I feel like telling everyone about me
  how great You are.
If only they could know the depths of Your love
  and Your eternal concern for those who
  will follow You!
But my songs are so often off-key.
My speech is so inadequate.
I simply cannot express what I feel,
 what I know to be true about Your love
  for Your creatures upon this world.

But even the songs of the birds
  proclaim Your praises.
The heavens and the earth beneath them,
 the trees that reach toward You,
 the flowers that glow in colorful beauty,
 the green hills and soaring mountains,
 the valleys and the plains,
 the lakes and the rivers,
 the great oceans that pound our shores,
 they proclaim Your greatness, O God,
 and Your love for the sons of men.

How glorious it is to be alive, O Lord!
May every breath of my body,
 every beat of my heart,
 be dedicated to Your praise and glory.

Psalm 93

It may not always be apparent,
   but God does reign over our world.
He rules in majesty and might,
   and no philosophy or power can cast
      Him from His throne.

He allows us to cross up His purposes—
   even to destroy His visible creation about us.

But His place and His reign are eternally secure.
And so are they who put their trust in Him,
   who live by His precepts,
      and who follow His course for their lives.

Psalm 94

It is difficult, O God, to understand
        how You can ignore Your enemies
    or fail to take action against them as they
        persist in thwarting Your purposes
        and abusing Your children upon this world.
They provoke me to anger, O Lord.
How can You withhold Your vengeance?

Even those of us who name Your name
        and sing Your praises
        are often indifferent to or careless about
        the needs of our fellowmen about us.
We stand indicted, Lord.
Our calloused self-centeredness has perpetuated
        the wars and poverty and bigotry
        that abound about us.
We don't hate these people, Lord.
We just don't really care about them.

Is it possible, O Lord, that we are Your enemies?
That we are thwarting Your purposes and abusing
        Your children upon this world?
We are busy with good works, Lord.
We build churches and send forth missionaries
        and establish schools and hospitals
        and homes for the elderly.
But we don't like the ghettos, Lord,
    or the people who can't speak our language
        or don't appreciate our patronizing gifts.
They frighten us when they reach out for what
        we have labored for,

our affluence, our respectability,
our right to be wealthy and comfortable
and secure.
Sometimes, Lord, we just don't like people.
Why don't they leave us alone
so we can love and serve You in peace?

Thank You, God, for not pouring out Your wrath
upon those who are disobedient to You.
We have been Your enemies.
Even while we worship
in our comfortable sanctuaries,
we have stood in Your way.
And thank You, God,
because You love even Your enemies,
and through Your chastisement may translate
them into sons.

Strike the scales from our eyes, O Lord,
that we may see Your handwriting on the wall
and accept Your chastening love
and return to You in repentance and in faith.
Strike the shackles from our hearts and hands
that we may reach out to demonstrate and to
relate Your love to Your children all about us.

Psalm 95

Let us begin this day with singing.
Whether we feel like it or not,
   let us make glad sounds
      and force our tongues to articulate words
      of thanksgiving and praise.

The facts are: God is with us;
   this world and we who live in it are
      in His hands;
   He loves us; He has adopted us as His children;
   we belong to Him.

This makes us valid, worthwhile.
We are truly significant in the eyes of our God,
      irrespective of our human feelings
      or the comments of our critics about us.

This isn't the way we feel this morning.
But this is the way it is.
We don't need the plaudits of our peers,
   for we have God's stamp of approval.

So let us begin this day with singing
   whether we feel like it or not.
Then we may end this day with praises,
   because we know — and may even feel —
      that we shall forever be the objects of
      God's concern and the children of His love.

Psalm 97

I can't even see the sun this morning.
The coastland fog has blotted out heaven's light,
   and the early hours are cold and damp.
But God is here—in me and around me,
   and I will rejoice in Him.

I hear no angel choirs.
There are no church bells to summon me to worship
     and meditation.
There are only the thunder of four-wheel vehicles
     and the acrid odor of exhaust,
   as men rush forth to their unnumbered shrines
     and pursue their avaricious goals.
But God is here—in me and around me,
   and I will rejoice in Him.

I cannot see the mountains or smell the flowers
     or even hear the song of birds.
I cannot feel love or concern from the people
     that bustle about me.
I see unhappiness and injustice and depravity.
I hear the ear-grating sounds of pain and complaint.
I feel the stifling pressures that suck me
     into that stream that rushes by my door.
But God is here—in me and around me,
     and I will rejoice in Him.

Our great God does care for His creatures.
He secures forever those who faithfully
     and lovingly relate to Him.
He is here—in us and around us.
Let us all rejoice in Him!

Psalm 99

The Lord does reign over this world!
Even when the earth quakes
    and the fires rage through the canyons
    and floods inundate the lowlands
    and men and their creations are laid low,
    God is Lord and Master over all the earth.

The Lord does reign over this world!
Even when men turn against one another
    and nations are engaged in war
    and violence and injustice are heaped
      upon His creatures,
    God is Lord and Master over all the earth.

God's creatures bear the consequences
      of their self-centeredness,
    and this world is distorted by their depravity.
But the Lord forgives those who turn to Him
    and makes them His children and His servants
    and through them seeks to heal this world's
      gaping wounds
      and the hurts that men inflict upon one another.

The Lord relates to those who call upon Him.
The priests and prophets of history heard
      His voice and followed in His course
      for their lives.
His servants and disciples of this hour
      sense His presence and communicate His love
      and grace to those who reach out for Him.

The Lord does reign over this world!
He is Lord and Master over all the earth!

Psalm 101

O God, I love those hymns that speak
    of loyalty and justice,
        those prayers for the deprived and oppressed,
        even while I deprive and oppress my fellowmen
            through my apathy and egocentricity.

I embrace the old creeds that tell of Your love
        and the commandments that instruct me
        to reflect that love to others —
    even while I turn inward and allow bigotry
        and prejudice to color my relationships
        to those outside my private little club.

I treasure those promises I made in the sanctuary,
    those vows and solemn pledges before the altar —
    even while I flirt with this world's gods
        and bow before man-made shrines.

I decry the distortions of our world,
    the poverty and pain and the indignities
        suffered by multitudes of this world's citizens —
    even while I stand aloof and wait for
        man's sorry needs to be met by others
        and brazenly oppose those remedies
        which may result in some personal deprivation.

I avoid the sinner and belittle the proud
        and stand clear of cheaters and liars
        and choose as my companions the qualified
        and respected members of my society.
And all the while I claim to be Your son
        and to walk in Your ways.

Have mercy upon me, O God,
    for I am a selfish and self-centered creature!

Psalm 104

O Lord, how great and all-powerful You are!
And how beautiful is the world You created
     for our habitation!

Even before man was brought forth from the dust,
    You prepared for him a place in which
       to live and grow.
And everything man saw about him
       reflected the beauty and power
       of the living God.

There was clean air.
Pure water from snowcapped mountains flowed
       through green valleys
       and gathered together to become great lakes.
The skies shone with a million lights.
The land brought forth flowers and fruits
       to delight the eye and palate of God's creature.
And every part of the land
       and the waters that covered the land
       and the skies that looked down upon the land
       were filled with uncountable forms of life;
     and the world was vibrant and alive.

Your power and Your beauty were spread throughout
    the universe,
    but it was only upon the heart of man
     that You imprinted Your image.
And this creature,
    in his short stay upon this world,
    was destined to be Your son and co-worker
     in the ever-continuing process of creation.

Your creative activity has never ceased.
It continues in and through the life
        of creature man.
Limited and fallible as man is,
    his mind and his hands are assigned
        to corral Your lifegiving energies
        and to direct them in controlling
        and replenishing the earth
        that life might be given and sustained
        throughout the world.

O Lord, how great and all-powerful You are!
And how beautiful is the world You created
        for our habitation!

Psalm 105

How great is my God,
    and how I love to sing His praises!
Whereas I am often frightened when I think about
       the future,
    and confused and disturbed by the rapidly
      changing events about me,
    my heart is secured and made glad
      when I remember
      how He has cared for me throughout the past.

When I was brought forth from my mother's womb,
    God's hand was upon me.
Through parents and people who cared,
    He loved and sheltered me and set me upon
      His course for my life.
Through illness and accident
      my God has sustained me.
Around pitfalls and precipices
      He has safely led me.
When I became rebellious and struck out on my own,
    He waited patiently for me to return.
When I fell on my face in weakness and failure,
    He gently set me upon my feet again.
He did not always prevent me from hurting myself,
    but He took me back to heal my wounds.
Even out of the broken pieces of my defeats
      He created a vessel of beauty and usefulness.

Through trials and errors, failures and successes,
    my God has cared for me.
From infancy to adulthood
    He has never let me go.

His love has led me — or followed me —
      through the valleys of sorrow and the
      highlands of joy,
   through times of want and years of abundance.
He has bridged impassable rivers
      and moved impossible mountains.
Sometimes through, sometimes in spite of me,
    He seeks to accomplish His purposes in my life.

He has kept me through the stormy past;
    He will secure and guide me through the
      perilous future.
I need never be afraid,
    no matter how uncertain may be the months
      or the years ahead of me.
How great is my God,
    and how I love to sing His praises!

Psalm 106

How I praise God today!
How exciting it is to be His son and servant!
What is so amazing to me is the manner in which
        He makes hay out of the straw and stubble
      of my feeble efforts and foolish errors.

This is the way God deals with all His children.
We have so often fallen away from His love
    and accepted His gifts without respect
      or concern for the Giver.
We spout with gratitude when some great deliverance
        has come our way:
    a successful surgery, a return to health,
    a financial bonus, a debt erased,
    a reconciliation with a loved one.
But when the crisis is over and calm is restored,
    we are back to our old tricks,
    walking in our old ways,
    pursuing our self-centered goals,
    with little concern about God's way
      and will for our lives.

We rejoice when God smiles upon us,
    and sound off about how good and gracious He is.
But when we meet up with hard times
    or become enslaved within the boredom of the
      daily routine,
    we relapse into grumbling and griping
      and act as if God were a million miles away.

How loving and patient is my God!
Even when I fail Him,
 He never fails to love and care for me.
I so often limit Him by my inability
  to really trust Him,
 my unwillingness to obey Him,
 by my apathy, my self-concern,
 or my pursuit of the foolish goals and
  ambitions of this life.
And yet my God never ceases to pursue me,
 to draw me back into His circle of love,
 and to carry out His purposes even through
  the failures and defeats of my life.

How I praise God today!
How I pray that He may find pleasure in my love
 for Him!

Psalm 108

My heart is glad today, O God,
    and I am determined to serve You!
I celebrate Your presence.
I glory in Your love for me.
I sing Your praises,
    and I desire to proclaim Your loving concern
        to all men about me.

The people that I travel with
        have little feeling for You.
They act as if You do not exist.
They are empty.
Their lives have little meaning or purpose.
They bounce about in a vacuum with the
        deepest longings of their hearts unfulfilled.

I know to whom I belong,
    and I know where I am going.
I know that You are my Lord
    and that You will accompany me as I walk
        the streets of the city and mingle
        with its groping inhabitants.

I pray, O Lord, that You will use me,
    that through my fumbling efforts
        You will touch some lonely soul with Your
        healing and love.

My heart is glad today, O God.
Grant that I may communicate to others
    some measure of this eternal joy.

Psalm 109

O God, I have been taught to believe
    that You are God over our world.
It has been dinned into my ears by the preachers
    of my youth
    and by parents and teachers and self-appointed
    apostles.
"God holds the reins," they say.
"He will have the last word," they claim.

I've honestly tried to believe it.
And with tongue in cheek
    I've sounded off to others about Your power
    and Your promises.
Maybe they sensed my incredulity.
It may be that they just habitually accepted
    or unthinkingly nodded assent
    to my platitudes and pronouncements.
How can I, O God, really believe
    in Your omnipotence
    unless I look the other way when tragedy
    befalls
    or close my eyes to the agony and ugliness
    on all sides of me?

I cannot believe that You inflict pain
    upon Your creatures.
I realize that our suffering is most often
    the consequences of our own selfishness.
But what about the babies born with two strikes
    against them?

the grizzly slaughter on battlefields
and highways?
the destruction of thousands when the earth
shifts and breaks up under them?
the pressures and indignities forced upon
minority races?
What about this, O God?
How can I explain this to my skeptical friends
or even to myself?

Is it possibly true, O God,
that You really are not omnipotent?
that this fractured world is not in the palm
of Your hand?
that Your great power is limited in respect
to this distorted planet and its
sin-ridden inhabitants?

O God, the basis of all being,
my ultimate and eternal concern,
I know that You are not floating out there
over and beyond our ball of clay.
You are in our world.
You are amongst Your creatures,
inscrutable, indefinable,
great in majesty and splendor.
You bring beauty out of ugliness.
Out of the ashes of our sickness and suffering
You bring forth new creations of joy
and loveliness.
I shall never want to define You, O God,
for I cannot worship what I comprehend.
But I pray for Your grace to stand firm even
in the midst of my nagging doubts
and to praise You in the midst of adversity.

Psalm 110

God spoke to me today.
He broke through my childish doubts
     with words of comfort and assurance.
"Hang in there; sit tight;
   stick to My course for your life," He said,
   "I will not let you down."

He reminded me of how He cared for past saints,
   how He watched over them and kept them
     through their hours of suffering
    and uncertainty.
He reviewed for me my own life,
   His loving concern through the days of my youth.
He restated for me my commission and appointment,
   His trust in me as His servant
    in this sorry world.
He reiterated His gracious promises to stand by me,
   to empower and support me in the conflicts
    that await me.

I know that God is with me today —
   just as surely as He was with His saints of old.
I have neither to fear nor to doubt
    the eternal love and presence of my Lord.

Psalms 114 and 115

We fear, O God, for our country
    and the tragic indifference that is demonstrated
        in respect to You and Your purposes.
We have built great shrines and memorials
        in Your honor.
We have established innumerable religions
        that presume to glorify and serve You.
We have respectfully imprinted Your name upon
        our coins and properly credited You in
        our founding principles.
Our leaders most generally call on You to guide them
        in the most critical decisions that they
        must make.
A remnant of our populace gathers occasionally
        to sing Your praises and profess its faith.
There are even special days when we count our
        blessings and conduct services of thanksgiving.

But the shrines we build do not always glorify You.
They often become soundproof fortresses that blot
        out the sounds of suffering that echo
        throughout the world about them.
Our numerous religions turn into vain attempts
        to box You into man-made ideas and
        concepts of divinity.
The coins which bear Your name are dedicated
        to the pursuit of our selfish ambitions and
        the acquisition of material wealth.
Our founding principles are interpreted in ways
        that benefit the powerful and oppress the weak.
Our laws sometimes contradict and oppose Your law

in respect to the consciences and convictions
    of Your children.
Our leaders call upon You to bless their intentions
    rather than to reveal Your plans
    in the government of men.
And those who do gather to sing Your praises
    are seldom committed to anyone or anything
    unless it is comfortable and convenient
    for their purposes.

And yet, O Lord, we pray
    that You will not give us up.
We have selfishly clutched at Your great blessings
    and abused the wealth You have put
    into our hands.
We have gathered for ourselves while
    countless millions
    of this world's creatures have died
    with their needs unfulfilled.
We have foolishly ignored You to worship the things
    that have come from Your hands.
We confess our rebelliousness and selfishness,
    O Lord,
  and pray that You will spare us.
Spare us, in order that you might renew us
    and save us
    and use us to channel Your blessings to Your
    children in every land.
You dealt mercifully with Your ungrateful children
    throughout history.
We pray that You will deal patiently and lovingly
    with us,
  that You will transform our words into actions
    and our shallow platitudes into genuine praises
  that will glorify and serve You in all the world.

Psalms 117 and 118

O God, I am thoroughly frightened when I see
     the things that are happening around me.
And when I dare to peer into the future,
     I become very nervous as I consider what may
     happen to me and my world.

I do remember Your many promises.
I keep telling myself:
   "With the Lord on my side I do not have
     to be afraid;
   what can man do unto me?"
But when I see the old foundations crumbling
     and the old certainties
     and securities giving way,
   I feel as if I am falling with no one
     to catch me,
   or that my ship has broken loose
     from its anchor,
     and I am at the mercy of a tempestuous sea.

Our world has slipped its moorings:
   our population threatens to overwhelm us;
   our waste products are about to smother us;
   our modern weapons are capable
     of obliterating us.
Because we are incapable of loving and living
     for one another,
   we are about to be destroyed by our own
     self-centeredness
   and to turn the beautiful world You have given us
     into a wasted and desolate planet.

It all seems so unreal,
and I feel so small and insignificant
in such a world.
And sometimes it seems, O God,
that even You have left us to our own devices
and have given us up for lost.
Or, I wonder, are You about to wind up history?
Is Your purpose for our world about
to be consummated?

You do speak to my fears, O Lord.
You offer no guarantees about the future
of the world,
but You have assured me that my status as
Your beloved child is eternal.
Whatever happens to my world,
You will never let me go.
You have set me free from fear and will keep me
safe and secure through all of the storms
that rage about me.
You are my God,
whatever happens to the world about me,
and I will celebrate Your love forever.

Psalm 119

O God, I want so very much to please You,
    to walk in Your ways
        and to carry out Your purposes.
There is nothing as important to me as being
        in the center of Your will
        and living within Your design for my life.

While others may find their fulfillment
        in the acquisition of wealth
        or the accumulation of things,
    in doing something better than everyone else,
        or in the plaudits of their peers,
    my foremost desire is to be the object
        of Your love
        and to be Your child and servant forever.

Not only have You fashioned me with Your hands,
        O Lord,
    and created me for Your purposes,
    You have stamped Your image upon my heart.
Therefore my deepest longings are met only in You
        and in the dedication of my life
        to the accomplishment of Your objectives.

How can I live a life that is pleasing to You,
        O Lord?
My instincts are earthbound.
The ephemeral delights of this life tantalize
        and tempt me.
My insatiable longings and desperate attempts
        to please You are thwarted by the innumerable
        enemies of my soul.

I fail so often to do what I really want to do,
    to attain what I strive for,
    to grasp what I reach for,
    and I fall back in shame and am flattened
    in despair.

You do forgive me when I fail, O Lord,
    and You put me upon my feet again.
You have promised to strengthen me
        and to sustain me in my daily conflicts.
Now I pray for the wisdom to discern Your will
        and the grace to carry it out in the difficult
        days before me.

You have shown me how much You love me, Lord;
    now show me how to love You.
Your standards for me are clear.
I am to translate Your love into terms that
        others can comprehend,
    to demonstrate it before my fellowmen about me.
I can truly love You only inasmuch as I proceed
        to love Your children in this world.
I can serve You only as I commit my life to service
        on behalf of my brothers and sisters.
I can offer sacrifices to You only by way
        of the altar of my neighbor's need.
This is Your law, Your standard,
    Your design and will for my life.
This is the way in which I will be pleasing to You.

I do love You, O God,
    and Your will for me is the delight of my heart.
I have a sincere love for many people who cross
        my path,
    and I rejoice in the privilege of serving them.

And yet, O Lord, there are so many people
        that I do not love.
The demons of bigotry and apathy and jealousy
            and selfishness plague my soul and numb
            my sensitivities and stay my hand from
            reaching out to help my fellowman.
I sin against You when I sin against them,
        and I need to be restored and renewed
            by Your loving touch.

How I praise You, O Lord,
        because You love me even when I fail
            to respond in loving obedience!
Whereas I cannot comprehend You,
        You do understand me,
        and You continue to hold me within Your
            loving embrace.
While I fall short of my sincere intentions
            to abide within Your will for me,
        Your promises are eternally secure;
        and You tenderly and patiently rekindle
            the fires within me and empower me to do
            that which I cannot do by myself.

I love You, O God,
        and I gladly accept Your will and purpose
            for my life.
Now bless me and guide me
            and grant me the grace to walk within that
            will and purpose
        and have the joy of knowing that I am pleasing to You.

Psalm 120

I am distressed, O Lord,
  by the attitudes and actions of those
    who claim to honor Your name
    and to live within Your purposes.

They don't really listen to Your Word.
They appear to be following some other god
  or are simply taking the path
    of least resistance.
They assume that their wishes are Your will,
  that the crowd they travel with
  or the nations that govern them
  are righteously carrying out Your objectives
    irrespective of their ungodly means
    and methods.

How long, O Lord, must I dwell in a world
    that breeds violence
  and amongst people that engage in war?

Teach me, O God, how to be a peacemaker,
  how to confront violence with love,
  how to courageously and patiently promote
    Your will and Your Word amongst the
    hostile and angry masses about me.

Psalms 122 and 123

How good it is to enter the sanctuary of the Lord!
I know that God is not confined within
        man's four-walled creations,
   nor is He attached to altars and brass symbols.
And yet, in the beauty and quietness of God's house
        I find His presence very real and fulfilling.

God is with me and about me
        even as I make my way through the concrete
        and steel jungles of the cold
        and unfriendly city.
He is present even behind the anonymous faces
        of the rushing crowds elbowing their way
        to their respective destinations.
I find Him in the hearts and lives of His children
        who infiltrate the urban masses
        and who are running His errands and fulfilling
        His purposes in the course of their daily duties.
I cannot outrun or evade my God.
He goes before me and follows closely behind me.
He will keep me and sustain me wherever I am.

And yet I rejoice as I enter His sanctuary
        and mingle with those who honor His name
        and seek His grace.
There, shielded from the screaming tensions
        and ear-splitting sounds of the city,
   in the company of those who love one another,
   I happily open my heart to the loving mercy
        of God.

Psalms 124 and 125

What cowards we are,
    we who claim to be the sons of God!
How insipid is our faith
        in an insecure and faithless world!

The pressures are increasing.
The old props are falling away.
Many of the old traditions and standards
        we held so dear are no longer relevant
        in our rapidly changing society.
Even the proclamations and exhortations,
    the prophecies and promises,
        that excited and supported us in our youth
        sound hollow and empty and frightfully inadequate
            in these times in which we live.
The little boxes which we wrapped around our God
        are breaking up;
    we can no longer hold on to Him
        in our expanding, exploding universe.

Though we cannot hold on to God,
        He does hold on to us.
Those who trust in the true God are more secure
            than the great mountains that rise above the
            clouds that cover us.
Though everything changes about us,
    our great God cannot be changed.
Though the sands may shift around us,
    even our institutions and governments
    and the ideals and aspirations of men,
        our great God is not subject to the impermanence
            of our temporal world.

Though the storm sweeps in upon us,
    our relationship to our loving God is forever.

What cowards we are, we who claim to be
        the sons of God!
We don't have to be afraid.
Let us have faith in God!

Psalm 126

Let us begin this day by rejoicing!
Let us acknowledge our Lord's love and concern
      and allow our bodies to break forth
      into happy hilarity!
Let us give our nerves and muscles the healthy
      exercise of laughter!
The Lord has done such wonderful things for us;
   let us be glad!

The day before us is uncertain.
We know not what we will encounter on our way.
While we rejoice with those who rejoice,
   we shall also weep with those who suffer.
While we may be surprised by ecstasy,
   we may also pass through corridors of darkness.
Wherever we go, we go forth as sons and servants
      of the living God,
    and we go forth to touch the lives of men
      with His healing love.
Let us begin this day with rejoicing,
   and return to our homes with gladness!

Psalm 129

O God, I get awfully tired of static.
I am fed up with the flack that comes my way
        from those I am trying to serve.
It seems that they suspect or misinterpret
        or question my motives or authority
        in respect to everything I do or say.
I think people enjoy putting me down.
I just can't get them off my back.

Do I have to perpetually live with this sort
        of thing, O Lord?
What about this joy that is promised to those
        who are Your servants and ministers?

Forgive me for my unworthy thoughts, O Lord.
Overlook my vicious complaints, and so fill
        my heart with Your love
        that I will respond in love even toward
        those who cannot love me.
Enable me, O Lord,
    to find my joy in You and to reflect that
        joy to the unresponsive, reactionary,
        disagreeable people who do not like me
        very much.

Psalm 132

We remember, O Lord,
  those past saints who suffered sorely
    on Your behalf.
In obedience to You they endured persecution —
  even torture and death.
In their heroic determination to live by Your will
      and to remain in Your course for their lives,
    they proclaimed and demonstrated Your Word
      to this world's masses.

We remember, O Lord,
  and we are ashamed of our insipid faith,
  our cowardice,
  our fear of offending those with power over us
    and of being despised by our fellowmen
    around us.

Make us aware, O Lord,
  of Your children who even today are suffering
    for their faith,
  who, even in our great country,
  have the courage to place Your will above
    the laws of the state
  and are subjected to the indignities
    of imprisonment,
  the scorn of their peers,
  and even the compassionless criticisms of many
    of us who honor Your name.

We confess, O Lord,
  our lack of courage and understanding.

We pray for Your blessing upon those who suffer,
that You will not forget them in their
hour of trial,
and that You will not turn Your face from them
in their lonely hours of doubt and pain.

Visit them with joy; empower them with Your Spirit;
watch over and care for them.
May the influence of their courageous convictions
shake us out of our lethargy,
move us from the fringes of fear and indecision
into the center of Your will,
and endue us with the grace to carry on Your
purposes in scorn of the consequences that
may come to our lives.

Psalm 135

Despite the depressing conditions of our world
  and the distortions of our society,
 or even the problems and conflicts of our lives,
 let us take time to praise the Lord.

We who gather for services of worship,
 let us come together to celebrate God's presence
  and to praise Him for His great gifts.
As we find our place in our workaday world,
 let us begin by praising the Lord.
When we meet with our family and friends,
 let us unite our voices in praises to the Lord.
The farmer who labors alone with the soil and seed
  can praise that God who brings forth
  the fruit.
The city dweller who mingles with the masses that
  impersonally jostle him
  and works amid the tall structures that
  belittle him
  can praise that God who knows and loves
  him forever.
Without our God to praise and worship and serve,
 there is no real purpose in life,
 no meaning, no identity, and no reason for
  existing in this cold, calculating world.
You who are on beds of pain,
 even you have reason to praise the Lord.
You who are left to die in homes for the aged,
 you, too, can find purpose in praising
  the Lord.

When you feel you are forgotten,
   your loving God never forgets.
When you are tired and lonely,
   your great God will never leave your side.

Those people who have no God to praise,
   who neglect to relate to their Creator
      and Redeemer,
   are like creatures wandering in darkness.
They focus upon the fitful, fleeing things
      of this life.
Like butterflies over a flower bed,
   they flutter from blossom to blossom,
   getting their honey wherever they can.
Then they return to their beds only to await the
      meaningless existence of another day.

God is available — to be recognized
      and to be praised.
He has reached out to His lost children
      to lovingly draw them to Himself.
He gives them identity and purpose,
   a name and a goal,
   and makes them eternally secure
      and significant.

Let us praise the Lord!
He makes our lives and our living,
   every hour and every day, truly worthwhile;
   and we belong to Him forever.

Psalm 136

Thank You, God,
    for all these things that reveal Your love.
Thank You for the heavens that cover us,
    for the earth beneath our feet,
    for the sun in the day and the stars of the night,
    for the snow and the rains and the rivers
        and the lakes,
    for mountains and valleys and trees and flowers.

Thank You, God,
    for those people who demonstrate Your love.
Thank You for those great men who followed You
        throughout history,
    for the priests and prophets and apostles
        and ministers,
    for doctors and teachers and mothers and fathers
        and painters and musicians and writers and
        farmers and laborers and clerks,
    for those men and women who accepted Your love
        and who dedicated their lives to loving
        their fellowman.

Thank You, God,
    for choosing me to be one of Your people,
    for calling me and equipping me to communicate
        Your love to my world about me.
Thank You, God.

Psalm 137

How grateful we are, O God,
    for our great country
    and for the blessings that You poured
        out upon our land!
How concerned we are, O God,
      that our very nation may become our god
        and that we worship the gifts rather than
        the Giver!

Is it possible, O God,
      that our laws may circumvent Your will?
      that our freedom may place chains on others?
      that our wealth may result in someone else's poverty?
      that our power may come by way of another's weakness?
      that our enemies may be those who are obedient to You?
Dare we pray, O God,
      that You take away those things that come
        between us and You?
      that You raise up men who will oppose
        those institutions
        and those citizens who carelessly,
        even unconsciously,
        equate loyalty to country
        with allegiance to You?

We do pray, O God,
      that our nation be restored to Your objectives
    and that Your children who abide in this land
        dedicate their lives to You and Your purposes
        throughout the world.

Psalm 140

O God, deliver our nation and our world
　　　　from those men in positions of authority
　　　　who resort to violence to carry out
　　　　their objectives.
They sweet-talk us into believing they are
　　　　acting in our interests,
　　and brainwash us into blind, flag-waving
　　　　allegiance,
　　until we march by their side
　　　　into bloody wars that decimate and destroy
　　　　our brothers and sisters in the family of man.

Deliver all of us, O Lord,
　　from the notion that anything of value or worth
　　　　can be obtained by hostile or violent actions.

Our God is on the side of those who are afflicted.
He will ultimately and justly deal with men
　　　　of violence,
　　and show His mercy upon the victims of their
　　　　obscene actions.

Help us, O Lord,
　　even at the risk of our lives and well-being,
　　to overcome hate with love
　　and to be peacemakers in a world that is
　　　　so racked and distorted by the atrocities
　　　　of war.

Psalm 141

O God, I come to You in sorrow and shame.
I spoke up in my own defense today
     and uttered words that knifed their way
     into the heart of my friend,
  and this created a great rift between us.
I would never raise my hand to strike him,
   but the tongue is more destructive than the fist,
   and I hurt that one whom I love.

Heal the hurt of my friend, O Lord,
   and heal the sickness within my heart
     that forced my foolish tongue
     into such irresponsible actions.

I come to claim Your loving mercy.
I pray, as well, that you grant my friend
     the grace to forgive me.
May Your Spirit who abides in my heart
     curb and control my rebellious tongue
  and teach me to speak words that give life
     and promote love in the hate-ridden world
     about me.

Psalm 143

It was another one of those days, Lord,
    when I should have stayed in bed.
Everything I attempted to do was destined for failure.
I honestly tried to show concern for my fellowman
       but got cold shoulders in return.
I tried to speak words of comfort,
    and they were thrown right back into my teeth.
I wanted to do well at my job,
    but it seemed I just got in everybody's way.

Sometimes it just isn't worth it, Lord,
    and I wonder if it isn't time to fold up
      and shove off in search of greener pastures.
I want desperately to be a success,
    to add points to my score,
    or to get commended now and then.
But this didn't happen today, Lord,
    and it happens so seldom that I wonder
      what is wrong with me.
Am I following Your course for my life?
    Or am I just muddling through without
      design or destination?

I need You, God,
    more than I ever needed You before.
And if I don't get some special lift,
    some sense of Your support and encouragement,
    I will go right down the tube.

Come in closer, O Lord,
    that I may hear again Your voice of comfort
      and concern.

Psalm 144

O God, it is difficult to understand
>> how You can regard man with such high regard
>> and show him so much concern.

His years upon this earth are so few.
He is little more than a wisp of wind
>> in the time and space of Your great universe.

You created him as the object of Your love —
>> only to see him turn from You
>> to play with his foolish toys.

You tried to teach him to love his fellowman —
>> only to see him express his fear and suspicion
>> and hate through cruel acts of violence and war.

You showered upon him Your abundant gifts —
>> only to see him make them his ultimate concern.

Still You continue to love him
> and seek incessantly to save him from destroying
>> himself and the world You have placed
>> in his hands.

Even while he rejects You,
> You reach out to draw him back to Yourself.

Even while he suffers the painful consequences
>> of his rank rebelliousness,
> You offer to him Your healing and demonstrate
>> Your desire to restore him to love and joy.

And when he finally turns to You,
> he finds You waiting for him,
> ready to forgive his sins and to reunite him
>> to Your life and purposes once more.

That man who returns to his God is happy indeed!
He will forever be the object of God's love
>> and blessings.

Psalms 147 through 150

How good it is to celebrate God's presence
    and to sing His praises throughout each day!
We celebrate what He has done for man
      through history:
    His creation of our world
      and the sun and the moon
      and the unnumbered
      stars that light up our universe;
    His creatures that swim and crawl and walk
      and fly upon our planet;
    His children destined to enjoy these great
      gifts about them.
We praise Him for dealing with creature man:
    through His blessings heaped upon him;
    His revelations through signs and wonders;
    His tender love and gentle concern in His
      caring for him.
We praise Him for His devoted servants:
    who communicated His Word;
    who performed His miracles;
    who brought His healing to men's hurts.
We celebrate His continued blessings to our world:
    the flowers that bloom in glorious color;
    the rains that freshen the earth;
    the birds that fill the air with song.
We give thanks for His perpetual love:
    His forgiveness of men's sin;
    His pursuit of those who run from Him;
    His reaching out to heal them and to draw
      them to Himself.

We call upon all men to praise the Lord:
    those who preach to proclaim His love;
    those who sing to glorify His name;
    those who can shout or whistle or write or paint
        or dance or play musical instruments or pound
        on drums or ring bells to join in celebrating
        the majesty of our great and loving God.